TRAGEDY IN DALLAS

The Story of the Assassination of John F. Kennedy

BY STEVEN OTFINOSKI

D0096258

Consultant:
Richard Bell, PhD
Associate Professor of History
University of Maryland, College Park

CAPSTONE PRESS
a capstone imprint

Tangled History is published by Capstone Press,
1710 Roe Crest Drive, North Mankato, Minnesota 56003
www.mycapstone.com

Library of Congress Cataloging-in-Publication Data
Tragedy in Dallas : the story of the assassination of John F. Kennedy /
by Steven Otfinoski.
pages cm.—(Tangled history)
Includes bibliographical references and index.
Summary: "In a narrative nonfiction format, follows people who experienced the
assassination of John F. Kennedy"—Provided by publisher.
ISBN 978-1-4914-8451-7 (library binding)
ISBN 978-1-4914-8455-5 (pbk.)
ISBN 978-1-4914-8459-3 (ebook pdf)
1. Kennedy, John F. (John Fitzgerald), 1917–1963—Assassination—Juvenile
literature. I. Title.
E842.9.O817 2016
973.922092—dc23   2015035083

Editorial Credits
Adrian Vigliano, editor; Heidi Thompson, designer; Tracy Cummins, media researcher;
Laura Manthe, production specialist

Photo Credits
AP Photo: 73; Corbis: Bettmann, Cover, 36, Tom Dillard/Dallas Morning News, 82;
Getty Images: Art Rickerby/The LIFE Picture Collection, 53, CBS Photo Archive,
11, Fotosearch, 6, Keystone France/Gamma Keystone, 94, Lee Lockwood/The LIFE
Images Collection, 101, Liaison Agency, 4; JFK Library: White House Photographs/
Robert L. Knudsen, 78; Library of Congress: Thomas J. O'Halloran, 15, Victor Hugo
King, 35; Wikimedia: NARA, 22, White House Photographs/Cecil W. Stoughton, 56

Printed in US.
007534CGS16

TABLE OF CONTENTS

FOREWORD

On Thursday, November 21, 1963, President John F. Kennedy and his wife, Jackie, said good-bye to their two children and left Washington, D.C. The Kennedys were flying to San Antonio at the start of a three-day tour through Texas. Before leaving, the president promised his son, John (known to the public as "John John"), that he would be back to celebrate John's third birthday on Monday.

The Texas trip was an important one for Kennedy. He

hoped to improve relationships between conservative and liberal Democrats in the state while gaining support for the upcoming 1964 election. Kennedy planned to run for a second term, and Texas held a large number of electoral votes he needed to win. Even though his vice president, Lyndon Johnson, was from Texas, there were strong anti-Kennedy feelings in the state, especially in the conservative city of Dallas. Kennedy hoped that he and Jackie could charm Texans on this trip and win some of them over.

Air Force One landed in San Antonio at 1:30 p.m. Vice President Johnson had also just arrived, but he waited with Texas Governor John Connally to greet the president. Afterward the Kennedys attended the dedication of the U.S. Air Force School of Aerospace Medicine at Brooks Air Force Base. Then they flew to Houston and the president spoke to the League of United Latin American Citizens at the Rice Hotel. Next the presidential party attended a dinner at the Sam Houston Coliseum. That night the Kennedys flew to Fort Worth, where a third motorcade took them to the Texas Hotel for a well-earned night's rest. The first day of the Texas tour had gone extremely well. So far the crowds had been enthusiastic and there was every reason to hope that people in Dallas would be just as friendly and welcoming when they met them the next day.

"WHAT'S IN THE PACKAGE, LEE?"

1

Marina and Lee Harvey Oswald

Lee Harvey Oswald

2515 West Fifth Street, Irving, Texas, November 22, 1963, 7:00 a.m. (Central Standard Time)

Lee Harvey Oswald dressed quietly, preparing for the day. Turning around, he saw that his wife, Marina, was awake and looking at him. He continued dressing in silence, knowing they had little to say to one another. Although he still spent time in Marina's home, their marriage, for all practical purposes, was over.

The house belonged to Ruth Paine, a good friend of Marina's. Oswald stayed at the house some nights to visit with his two daughters, but yesterday he had found himself an unwelcome guest. He usually came on a Friday night, but this time showed up on a Thursday instead. Marina was not pleased, and all his pleading with her to get back together only seemed to harden her resolve to keep him away.

At 24 years of age, Oswald had felt like a misfit for as long as he could remember. Now he seemed to be facing nothing but dead ends in his life. A former Marine, he defected to the Soviet Union in 1959, hoping to find a better life there under Communism. But the government gave him a boring factory job in Minsk, and he quickly became disillusioned with the Communist system.

When Oswald met Marina at a dance in 1961, it seemed like the best thing to happen to him during his time in Russia. They were married six weeks later. He returned to the United States with Marina in 1962. By then they had a daughter, June, but their marriage was falling apart. Oswald was disappointed by how quickly Marina fell in love with America and its materialism. He knew that she could not forgive his inability to support her and June financially. Marina soon began living with Paine, a Quaker who wanted Marina to teach her Russian.

Oswald had reached a crossroads in his life. He was stuck in a poor-paying job packing textbooks at the Texas School Book Depository—a job Paine helped him get. He had little hope of earning enough money to support his family, which now included a second daughter, one-month-old Audrey. He was reaching the end of his rope.

Oswald finished dressing as Marina fed the baby. He went out into the garage to retrieve the rifle he had left there, wrapped in a blanket. He put the weapon into a long, brown paper package he had fashioned at work. Then, stepping back into the house, he removed his wedding ring, placed it in a china cup, and left $187 on the bureau. With the package under his arm, Oswald left the house and walked the half block to the home of his coworker, Buell Frazier.

As they climbed into Frazier's beat-up Chevy, Frazier glanced over his shoulder. "What's in the package, Lee?" he asked.

"Curtain rods," replied Oswald, hoping the rifle's disguise would fool Frazier.

Frazier nodded. "How come you aren't bringing a lunch to work?" he asked.

"I'm going to buy it," Oswald said.

His real plan for the lunch hour did not involve eating, but that was no one else's business. As the two men headed for downtown Dallas, the morning's light rain began to fall more steadily from the cold, gray sky.

Bob Schieffer
The Schieffer home, Fort Worth, 7:45 a.m.

Twenty-six-year-old Bob Schieffer pulled his two-seat Triumph sports car into his mother's driveway and wearily went inside the house. He was used to keeping late hours as the night police reporter at the *Fort Worth Star-Telegram*, but this had been an especially long night. He had left the office in the early morning and arrived at the Press Club around 2:00 a.m. The club was open to accommodate the White House press corps. They were part of the presidential entourage that had just come to town. Kennedy's visit to Fort Worth was a big story, but Schieffer was just a police

Bob Schieffer

reporter and wouldn't be assigned to the presidential beat. If he couldn't cover the president, he decided, at least he could mix with the big-name reporters who were on the story.

Sometime in the wee hours, the reporters decided to leave the Press Club for an after-hours club called the Cellar. Schieffer and one of his editors became their guides. They were soon joined at the Cellar by several off-duty Secret Service agents looking for some relaxation.

By the time the group left the club, the sun was coming up. Schieffer's mother and younger brother, Tom, were planning to go to the Texas Hotel that morning to catch a glimpse of Kennedy as he left for the airport and his flight to Dallas. But Schieffer had no intention of joining them. He'd enjoy a good sleep, and by the time he awoke the president would be long gone.

The day was not getting off to a good start for the vice president. Yesterday he had been publicly humiliated by a fellow Texan, liberal Senator Ralph Yarborough. On two separate occasions Johnson had invited the senator to ride with him in his car in the motorcade, and twice Yarborough had ignored the invitation and ridden with someone else. He was no friend of the conservative Johnson. Now Johnson sat staring at the front page of the *Dallas Morning News* where the headline used big, bold letters to declare: "YARBOROUGH SNUBS LBJ." Now everyone could read about this embarrassing incident in the paper.

The vice president thought about the feud that divided liberal Texas Democrats, like Yarborough, and more conservative

Democrats, such as Johnson himself. This division was one reason Kennedy had made the trip to Texas. But he and Johnson were also gathering votes, preparing for the fast-approaching 1964 election. The election was yet another source of concern weighing on his mind.

Johnson was well aware of the rumors that Kennedy would dump him from the ticket in 1964. While he feared this, at the same time he didn't exactly relish the thought of being vice president for another term. Johnson had given up a powerful position as Senate Majority Leader to take the office. As vice president he had become the powerless butt of many White House jokes.

Johnson had taken the job in part because it could eventually lead to the presidency after Kennedy's potential second term was over. But now he found himself competing for power with the president's brother, Robert. Robert, or "Bobby," as he was called, was the nation's attorney general and harbored presidential ambitions of his own.

The vice president shook off these worrisome thoughts and put on his raincoat and hat. He would join Kennedy and Governor Connally for a rally in the damp parking lot across the street, where a large crowd of union members was gathering. It would be Johnson's role, as usual, to introduce the president. Another thankless task for the number-two man.

As Senate Majority Leader from 1955 to 1961, Lyndon Johnson held a great deal of power in Washington, D.C.

Abraham Zapruder

As Abraham Zapruder entered the office, his secretary, Lillian Rodgers, greeted him. "Where's your camera?" she asked.

"It's raining," Zapruder replied. "It'll spoil the filming."

Zapruder, owner of a women's garment factory, was an avid home moviemaker. A transplanted New Yorker, he was also an enthusiastic Democrat and Kennedy admirer. He had been planning for days to film the presidential motorcade, scheduled to come through nearby Dealey Plaza around noon.

Rodgers pointed out the window. The rain clouds had given way to sunshine, and she urged him to go back for his camera. "How many times will you have a crack at color movies of the president?" she asked.

Zapruder had to admit that it was an opportunity he wouldn't have again. He turned around and went home for the camera.

Nellie Connally
Texas Hotel, Fort Worth, 9:05 a.m.

Nellie Connally, wife of Governor John Connally, couldn't be more pleased with how things were going. This was the first time a Texas governor had played host to a sitting president, and her husband had planned every moment carefully. The crowds in San Antonio and Fort Worth had been warm and enthusiastic toward the young president. But the next destination, Dallas, was likely to be a different story.

Dallas was a conservative stronghold, and its citizens had vocally disapproved of the liberal Kennedy. Connally feared that the results of the visit could be embarrassing. Only a month earlier, U.S. ambassador to the United Nations Adlai Stevenson, a Kennedy supporter, had been attacked during a visit to Dallas. She prayed that no such incident would mar the president's visit.

Connally finished dressing and headed downstairs to the Chamber of Commerce breakfast about to begin in the Grand Ballroom. She entered the ballroom to find it packed by wall-to-wall tables that seated nearly 3,000 people who had come to hear Kennedy speak. But someone was missing from the head table. Jackie Kennedy, the president's wife, was not there. Was the First Lady ill? Connally hoped not. She didn't want anything to spoil this memorable visit.

Clint Hill

Texas Hotel, Fort Worth, 9:10 a.m.

In the two years he had served and guarded Jackie Kennedy, Secret Service agent Clint Hill had come to respect and admire her. Now, at his security post, he received a troubling phone call. It was agent Bill Duncan, calling from downstairs. "Clint," he said, "the president wants you to bring Mrs. Kennedy down to the breakfast—*now!*"

Hill entered the presidential suite. Jackie was dressed in her pink outfit, but showed no sign of being ready to go anywhere. When he delivered the president's request, the First Lady reluctantly agreed to accompany him downstairs.

He could understand why she might want to bow out of the event. This was the first time since her husband had become president that she had accompanied him on a domestic campaign tour. Hill knew it had to be exhausting. On top of that, he knew she was still recovering from the loss of the couple's second son, Patrick, who had died on August 9, 39 hours after being born.

As Hill and the First Lady entered the ballroom, the entire room burst into applause. He heard someone say, "Oh, isn't she lovely?" The president grinned as Jackie took her place at the head table.

After the breakfast, Hill and Roy Kellerman, the president's personal Secret Service agent, escorted the first couple back to their suite. Once the Kennedys were gone, the two agents went over the details of the upcoming motorcade trip. The plan involved traveling from the Dallas airport, Love Field, to the Trade Mart where the president would speak at a luncheon. The presidential limousine had been flown to Dallas and would be waiting for them at Love Field.

The limo had a Plexiglas bubble top that could be attached in case of bad weather. This job would fall to the limo's driver, agent Sam Kinney. Kellerman reminded Hill that Kennedy didn't like using the bubble top because he felt that it came between him and the public. He believed people wanted to feel close to their president at these moments. But, Hill reasoned, if the weather was rainy, as it was in Fort Worth, Kennedy would have less reason to object to the bubble top. Kellerman called the advance agent in Dallas for a weather report. He said the skies were clearing and the sun was shining.

Kellerman turned to Hill. "Tell Sam, top off," he said.

Lee Harvey Oswald steadily packed schoolbooks into cartons. As he worked, his gaze kept traveling to the southeast corner of the sixth floor, where the cartons were stacked in big piles. The floor had been cleared to allow the maintenance crew to replace the old floorboards, long in need of renovation. The box piles would serve as a perfect camouflage as he made his preparations.

The boxes hid the southeast window, which Oswald expected would provide an excellent view of the motorcade as it passed down Elm Street through Dealey Plaza. He carefully unwrapped the brown paper package he'd brought along and removed from inside a bolt-action 6.5 mm Italian rifle with a telescopic lens. He had bought the weapon through the mail from a Chicago sporting goods company for $21.45. Oswald had learned how to shoot in the Marines and had proved a good marksman. In just two hours he would put his marksmanship to the ultimate test.

"YOU CAN'T SAY THAT DALLAS DOESN'T LOVE YOU."

2

The Kennedys received a warm welcome upon their arrival at Love Field in Dallas.

Clint Hill

Agents Hill and Kellerman accompanied the Kennedys past an enthusiastic crowd of well-wishers to the waiting cars for the 30-minute drive to Carswell Air Force Base. There they would board Air Force One for the short flight to Dallas. It would be far simpler and cheaper, Hill felt, to drive by car from Fort Worth to the Trade Mart in Dallas. But White House staff wanted one more photo op for the newspapers. More exposure would be provided if the president took his motorcade from Love Field through downtown Dallas to the Trade Mart.

Motorcades made Hill nervous. But he tried to shake off his nerves and keep his mind focused on the job. It was essential to remain vigilant and fulfill his job of protecting the president and first lady.

Nellie Connally

Nellie Connally was not riding with her husband to Carswell. Instead, she found herself in the car with the Johnsons and Senator Yarborough. Connally wondered how Yarborough had finally been persuaded to accept the vice president's invitation to ride. She imagined President Kennedy had something to do with it.

Of course, Connally had heard about Yarborough snubbing the vice president yesterday, but she didn't relish the thought of getting involved and trying to become a peacemaker. Instead of sitting between the two men, she rode up front next to one of the Secret Service agents. It was a quiet ride. The vice president and senator sat in stony silence in the backseat. They finally arrived at Carswell to find another large crowd. Connally hoped the crowd would be as large and as friendly when they landed at Love Field.

Lyndon Johnson

The vice president's plane touched down several minutes ahead of Air Force One. Johnson knew the routine all too well. He and his wife, Lady Bird, would disembark and then wait to greet the Kennedys as they descended from their plane. It was, Johnson felt, rather silly, considering they had all been traveling together for the past two days.

Johnson had insisted that they travel by motorcade from the airport through the city instead of driving directly to the Trade Mart. He wanted to show the world that, even in the supposedly anti-Kennedy stronghold of Dallas, the president was loved. But Johnson expected his real moment to come that night when they left the gala fund-raiser dinner in Austin and arrived at his ranch outside town. He and Lady Bird would host the Kennedys for the night and all day Saturday. It would show the world that the president and vice president were close and, hopefully, quiet the rumors of Kennedy planning to drop Johnson as his running mate.

Air Force One glided into the airport, and Johnson shook Kennedy's hand as he left the plane. Earle Cabell, the mayor of Dallas, was there to greet the president. The mayor's wife gave the First Lady a large bouquet of red roses. A cheering crowd pressed up against the chain link fence and Johnson watched the president move from the waiting limousine toward the fence. Jackie quickly followed him. They shook hands and exchanged greetings with the crowd.

Johnson took Lady Bird's hand and headed for the crowd. But he soon realized that the people were only interested in the first couple. The Johnsons quickly retreated to their car. After a few minutes, the Kennedys returned and the motorcade began to move. The Connallys had the honor of riding in the presidential limo, while Johnson again had to endure the company of Senator Yarborough. Lady Bird sat between the two men and tried to make conversation, despite the silence between Johnson and Yarborough.

Rufus Youngblood, Johnson's Secret Service agent, rode up front with the driver. After a few minutes, the vice president's car joined the motorcade, heading slowly toward downtown Dallas.

Lee Harvey Oswald

Texas School Book Depository, Dallas, 11:45 a.m.

Oswald waited patiently for the other workers to leave the building for lunch. Many were going to watch the president's motorcade pass by. Oswald, convinced he was alone on the sixth floor, went to get his rifle. Suddenly he heard the rickety elevator stop and footsteps approaching.

It was fellow worker Charles Givens. "Forgot my cigarettes," Givens said, going for the pocket of his jacket. Then he turned back to Oswald. "Boy, aren't you coming downstairs?" he asked. "It's near lunchtime."

"No, sir," Oswald replied politely.

He asked Givens if he would close the gate of the west elevator so he could summon it up later. Givens agreed. Alone again, Oswald gazed out the open window. A large crowd was gathering along Dealey Plaza, a grassy, open area. Oswald looked at his watch. The presidential motorcade was due to pass in about half an hour.

Clint Hill

Love Field, Dallas, 11:55 a.m.

As the motorcade pulled out of the airport, Agent Hill walked alongside the presidential limo next to where the First Lady sat. Agent Bill Greer, a jovial Irishman and a Kennedy favorite, was at the wheel. Agent Kellerman sat beside him. Hill noted that one car ahead of the president's was driven by Dallas Police chief Jesse Curry.

The presidential limo was a long blue Lincoln, specially rebuilt and enlarged. It had two jump seats in the middle and elevated seats in the rear so that Americans could get a better view of their president. The car was equipped with running boards and steps in the back for Secret Service agents to stand on.

As the motorcade picked up speed, Hill fell behind. He jumped onto the running board of the Secret Service car, known as Halfback, which was directly behind the president's limo. Three other agents stood on the running boards with Hill, while presidential aides Ken O'Donnell and Dave Powers rode in jump seats. Hill turned to see the vice president's car directly behind. Bringing up the rear were the press cars.

As they drew closer to downtown, Hill noticed that the crowds were growing larger. He scanned the crowds with a sharp eye, looking for any sign of troublemakers or anything unusual. He'd be glad when the motorcade ended and they reached the Trade Mart.

Merriman Smith

Reporter Merriman Smith of United Press International (UPI) was feeling lucky. On each day of the president's Texas trip, four reporters from the press pool were chosen to ride in the press car and have close access to the president. Today Smith was one of them. He was a veteran White House correspondent and, as such, he felt he deserved the honor.

When the four reporters entered the car, Smitty, as he was known to his colleagues, took the front seat, where the radio telephone was located. Crammed into the backseat were Jack Bell of the Associated Press (AP), Bob Clark of ABC News, and Robert Barber of the *Dallas Morning News*.

Short, stocky Abe Zapruder knew he'd have a hard time filming the president over the heads of the people in the crowd. Because of this, he arrived early at the plaza to set up his camera. He was accompanied by his receptionist, Marilyn Sitzman, who came to help him.

Zapruder set up on a low concrete abutment that lay near the triple underpass into which the motorcade would move as it left Dealey Plaza. As he fidgeted with his zoom lens, he turned to Sitzman and tried to kid around with her. But the joking did not entirely soothe his nervousness. He assumed he would only have a few precious seconds to catch the passing motorcade on film and he didn't want anything to go wrong.

The knots of people lining the streets grew larger as the motorcade drew toward downtown. At one point they passed a young man holding up a sign that read: "PLEASE MR. PRESIDENT STOP AND SHAKE OUR HANDS!" To Hill's alarm, the president had Agent Greer stop the car. Kennedy stood up as the man with the sign and the people around him rushed forward to greet him.

As the motorcade resumed, Hill moved up and jumped on the rear of the president's limousine. The president turned and looked at him without speaking. Hill knew Kennedy didn't like him doing that. He wanted to avoid agents coming between him and the public. But Hill stayed where he was. The president had a job to do, but so did Hill.

Advertising editor John Newnam listened patiently as Jack Ruby chattered away on a variety of topics. Although not a big spender, Ruby, a local nightclub owner, was a steady advertiser with the paper, and Newnam felt obliged to hear him out. Ruby was in the process of complaining about the full-page, anti-Kennedy ad that had appeared in that day's edition. It angered Ruby for two reasons. One, he was an admirer of the president, and two, the ad was signed by one "Bernard Weissman." Ruby explained that "Weissman" sounded Jewish. He felt the man's ad would reflect badly on all Jews, including Ruby himself.

Finally, to Newnam's relief, Ruby got back to business. He wrote out a check in the amount of $36.87 for ads for his nightspots, the Carousel Club and the Vegas Club.

Taking the check, Newnam was dismayed to realize that Ruby still wasn't finished talking. Now he began explaining how he wouldn't stand for troublemakers in his clubs and that he knew how to defend himself. He boasted about a .38 revolver that he always carried with him. Finally, he seemed to be finished. As he walked away Newnam wondered why, as such a great admirer of the president, Ruby wasn't out watching Kennedy's motorcade drive past just a few blocks away.

Nellie Connally

Presidential motorcade, Dallas, 12:28 p.m.

Nellie Connally couldn't have been happier. The sun was shining, the crowds were cheering, and the most powerful man in the world was sitting only a few inches behind her in the limo. She had never seen his wife, Jackie, so relaxed.

Now they approached the last turn onto Elm Street. Connally knew they would then head into the triple underpass that would take them onto Stemmons Freeway and to the Trade Mart. But before that, Connally wanted the president to know how pleased she was with how well the visit was going. "Mr. President," she said, turning to him, "you can't say that Dallas doesn't love you!" The smile on Kennedy's youthful face widened as the limo's driver slowed down and made a careful turn.

The Kennedys and the Connallys greeted crowds of supporters as the motorcade made its way through Dallas.

"MY GOD, THEY ARE GOING TO KILL US ALL!"

3

Abraham Zapruder

Abe Zapruder stared at the president through the zoom lens of his Bell and Howell. Kennedy looked almost close enough to touch. Zapruder followed the car's movement, swinging the camera to the right. Then suddenly a freeway sign obscured the view. As the car reappeared, Zapruder saw a strange look come into the president's eyes and his hands go for his throat. For a moment he thought that Kennedy, who had a keen sense of humor, was mocking his own death. It was as if he was saying, "Oh, they got me." An instant later it was all too clear that this was no act. As Zapruder looked on in horror, he saw part of Kennedy's head explode. "They killed him! They killed him!" he screamed over and over as the camera continued to roll.

Having moved back to Halfback, Agent Hill stood on the running board, scanning the crowd. Suddenly he heard a loud noise behind him. He looked ahead and saw Kennedy put his hands to his throat and fall leftward. Hill leaped off Halfback and sprinted for the president's car. There was a second shot. Hill was almost on the car when a third shot rang out. It sounded to him like the sound of a melon shattering onto concrete.

At that moment blood sprayed his face, hair, and clothes. Still running, he grabbed a handhold on the rear of the limo. The car lurched forward, Hill's feet still on the pavement. He managed to pull himself up onto the rear of the limo as it sped forward. Looking up he saw Jackie Kennedy, on hands and knees, climbing back onto the trunk.

Good God, he thought, *She's going to go flying off the back of the car!* He grabbed her and pushed her back into the seat. As he did, the president's body fell to the left onto her lap. "Get us to a hospital!" he cried to Agent Greer, who was driving.

Nellie Connally
Presidential motorcade, Dallas, 12:30 p.m.

Nellie Connally turned to see the look of stunned surprise in Kennedy's eyes as he seized his throat.

"No, no, no!" she heard her husband cry, the same surprised look in his eyes. "My God," he yelled, "they are going to kill us all!" Then he slumped down in the seat. Connally pulled him into her lap, just as a third shot came.

From behind she heard Jackie shriek, "They've killed my husband!"

Connally was terrified that her husband was dead too. But now he stirred in her arms. Her husband was alive. As the limo picked up speed, she pulled his right arm over his chest. "Be still," she whispered. "It is going to be all right."

Even as she said it she felt in her heart that nothing would ever be right again.

Lyndon Johnson
Presidential motorcade, Dallas, 12:31 p.m.

Vice President Johnson heard the gunfire. Before he could react, agent Youngblood was facing him in the seat ahead and shouting, "Get down! Get *down!*"

In a flash, Youngblood yanked him down to the car floor, rolled over the seat, and fell on top of him. The agent's knees and elbows pressed hard on Johnson's back and all he could see were his wife's shoes and legs.

"Close it up! Close it up!" Youngblood yelled at the driver.

On the agent's shortwave radio Johnson heard a voice saying, "He's hit! Hurry, he's hit!" He knew the voice must be talking about the president.

Lee Harvey Oswald

Lee Harvey Oswald carefully hid his rifle between two rows of boxes. Unable to use the elevator, he rushed down the stairwell to the second floor. As he entered the workers' lunchroom he ran into his supervisor, Roy Truly, and a motorcycle officer who appeared to be asking questions about the shooting. The officer looked sharply at Oswald. "Come here," he said, drawing his revolver. "Do you know this man?" he asked Truly. "Does he work here?" Truly said he did. The officer nodded, turned away, and Oswald made his escape from the building.

As he ran out the front entrance, Oswald was stopped by a man who he took for a Secret Service agent. "Where's the phone?" the man asked. Oswald directed him into the building and headed down the street.

As a target shooter, Merriman Smith knew guns. When he said that was gunfire, the other reporters in the car believed him. He could see a flurry of activity in the Secret Service car ahead. The vehicle had only stopped for a few seconds, but the pause felt like a lifetime.

Smith composed his thoughts for a minute and then reached for the radio phone. He called the UPI Bureau in Dallas. "Three shots were fired at the motorcade … " Smith dictated. In moments, the teletype operator was dashing out a five-bell bulletin. Smith realized the bulletin was likely the first word to the world of the tragedy:

DALLAS, NOV. 22 (UPI)—THREE SHOTS WERE FIRED AT PRESIDENT KENNEDY'S MOTORCADE IN DOWNTOWN DALLAS.

From the backseat of the car, Jack Bell called out, "Smitty, you have had your turn, give it to me now." As the press car sped after the two cars ahead of it, Smith and Bell grappled for the phone. By the time Bell got it, the line had gone dead. The car came to a screeching halt at the Parkland Memorial Hospital emergency room entrance and everyone tumbled out.

Clint Hill

Parkland Memorial Hospital, Dallas, 12:39 p.m.

As the presidential limo arrived at the emergency room entrance, Hill and other Secret Service agents were ready to rush the stricken president inside. But Jackie Kennedy held her husband tightly in the blood-drenched backseat.

"Mrs. Kennedy, please let us help the president," pleaded Hill. But she only released her hold when Hill covered the president's head and upper torso with his suit coat. Then, with Kellerman and two others, Hill lifted the limp body onto a waiting hospital gurney. Jackie followed them into Trauma

Room 1, where doctors frantically went to work on the president. Hill tried to take her out into the hallway, but again she wouldn't budge. Kellerman asked Hill to call the White House to tell them the terrible news.

As he waited for the phone, Jackie agreed to leave the room with him. They sat outside in the hallway, staring at each other in complete silence. Then Kellerman handed Hill the phone. After Hill spoke briefly with an agent at the White House, a familiar voice came on the line. It was the president's brother, Bobby Kennedy.

"Clint, what's going on down there?" Kennedy asked.

Hill explained haltingly that the president had been very seriously injured.

"What do you mean seriously injured? How bad is it?" Kennedy demanded.

Hill paused before speaking. "It's as bad as it can get," he said.

Lee Harvey Oswald

Oswald was on the move. He caught a bus seven blocks from the depository, but he got off shortly after boarding. A few minutes later he got into a cab at the Greyhound bus station. He had the cabbie drop him off a short walk from his rooming house.

Bob Schieffer

The Schieffer home, Fort Worth, 1:00 p.m.

Bob Schieffer was rudely awakened from a sound sleep by his brother Tom. The urgent look in his brother's eyes stunned him.

"Kennedy has been shot—you'd better get to work!" Tom shouted.

Schieffer quickly threw on some clothes and reached for the snap-brimmed hat that made him look like a police detective. Then he hopped into his Triumph and sped downtown. On the radio he heard the terrible news—the president had been shot. *Why did something like this have to happen*, he thought, *and why did it have to happen in Texas?*

Lyndon Johnson
Parkland Memorial Hospital, Dallas, 12:40 p.m.

Vice President Lyndon Johnson was hustled out of his car by Secret Service agents, into the hospital, and down a series of corridors. They stopped at a room containing three cubicles. The agents yanked a surprised nurse and her patient out of the third cubicle. Johnson and Lady Bird were deposited in the small room where they would remain until the president's condition was known. Someone said that agent Youngblood should phone his superiors in Washington. "I'm not leaving this man to phone *anyone*," he replied. Johnson appreciated Youngblood's concern. Whoever shot the president might be gunning for him as well. Rumors of a widespread conspiracy were in the air.

Minutes dragged by. Lady Bird sat in a chair while Johnson stood. Neither spoke a word to one another. After a time, Secret Service agent Emory Roberts came in from visiting Trauma Room 1 and said that he didn't think the president would make it. He and other agents urged Johnson to let them take him back to Air Force One where they could immediately leave for the safety of Washington.

"No," said Johnson. "I'm not leaving until I have more definite news of the president's condition."

Earlene Roberts

1026 N. Beckley Avenue, Dallas, 1:00 p.m.

Housekeeper Earlene Roberts was watching news of the president's shooting on television when Lee Harvey Oswald came rushing into the roominghouse. "Oh, you are in a hurry," she said.

Oswald hustled past her without a word and went straight to his small $8-a-week room on the first floor. He returned a few moments later wearing a white zipper jacket over his work shirt. Roberts stared as he rushed past her again and out the door. She wondered why he was in such a hurry. She shook her head and returned to watching the grim events unfold on the television.

Nellie Connally

Parkland Memorial Hospital, Dallas, 1:10 p.m.

Nellie Connally had never felt as alone as she did waiting outside the room where doctors were working to save her husband's life. The doctors told her that John had been struck in the back. The bullet had penetrated his ribs and sent bone fragments into one lung before passing through his wrist and lodging in his left leg.

As she waited tensely for word of her husband's condition, a nurse came out of Trauma Room 2. She dropped something into Connally's hand.

It was one of her husband's gold cufflinks, fashioned from a Mexican peso. The other cufflink had been shot off by the gunman.

Lee Harvey Oswald

10th Street and Patton Avenue, Dallas, 1:15 p.m.

Lee Harvey Oswald was on the run without a clear escape plan. He was walking down Patton Avenue when a patrol car pulled up behind him. Inside was a lone police officer. When Oswald crossed the street, the patrol car pulled up alongside him and the officer spoke through the car's window. He asked Oswald some questions about who he was and where he was going.

Oswald fingered the .38 snub-nosed revolver in his jacket pocket that he had retrieved from his room at the roominghouse. He tried to answer the officer's questions. Unsatisfied, the officer got out of the car. He had taken no more than two steps when Oswald pulled out his gun and fired. He shot the man four times. The officer crumpled to the ground and lay still. Oswald heard voices. People on the street had seen the shooting. He began to run, unloading the empty shells from his revolver as he crossed a lawn. As he ran past two witnesses he muttered, "Poor dumb cop."

Lyndon Johnson
Parkland Memorial Hospital, Dallas, 1:20 p.m.

Kennedy aide Ken O'Donnell came into Johnson's cubicle. The grim news was written all over his ashen face.

"He's gone," was all he said.

"We've got to get in the air," said agent Roberts. Others voiced their agreement.

"Well, what about Mrs. Kennedy?" Johnson asked.

Someone said she could follow later, in another plane with the president's body. But Johnson said no. He agreed to leave for Air Force One now, but wouldn't leave the ground until Jackie arrived.

Just then Assistant Press Secretary Malcolm Kilduff came into the small room. "Mr. President," he said, addressing Johnson, "I have to announce the death of President Kennedy to the press. Is it all right with you?"

"No, Mac," Johnson replied. "Wait until I get out of here and back to the plane before you announce it." He still feared there could be a conspiracy and that he, and others in the government, would be the next targets. Johnson turned and nodded to the Secret Service agents. They sprang into action, escorting the Johnsons through the back doors and hallways of the hospital to unmarked cars waiting to take them to the Love Field airport.

Merriman Smith

It had been a frustrating hour for Merriman Smith. Upon arriving at the hospital, he had sent a further bulletin to UPI that reflected his lack of hard information about the shooting. The bulletin read:

FLASH FLASH
KENNEDY SERIOUSLY WOUNDED
PERHAPS SERIOUSLY PERHAPS
FATALLY BY ASSASSIN'S BULLET

Along with a crowd of other reporters, Smith had been waiting impatiently in an office for further developments. He now stood in the hallway, dictating more details over the phone to UPI. Suddenly he saw Malcolm Kilduff and Wayne Hawks of the White House staff rush by. He threw down the phone and raced after them.

Smith followed Kilduff and Hawks into a conference room. Kilduff faced the gathered reporters, one trembling hand holding a cigarette and the other a small scrap of paper.

"President John Fitzgerald Kennedy died at approximately one o'clock Central Standard Time today here in Dallas. He died of a gunshot wound in the brain," he said.

Malcolm Kilduff announced Kennedy's death after receiving confirmation that Johnson had reached Air Force One.

Julia Postal

Julia Postal was running the ticket booth at the Texas Theatre when the manager of the nearby shoe store stepped up to her window. He told her he'd just seen a suspicious character sneak into the theater. "You'd better call the police," he said. She did so, immediately.

The officer who answered informed Postal that they were investigating two homicides, one right nearby. "We have your man," she said. She proceeded to detail Oswald from the manager's description and his suspicious behavior. The officer thanked her and hung up.

Within minutes a large number of police cars descended on the theater. At least 15 officers rushed inside. Postal had never seen anything like it. It was just like in a movie.

In the dark of the theater, Oswald sat next to a couple as a war movie lit up the screen. He would hide here and plan his next move. Suddenly the house lights came up and police officers flooded down the aisles. Before Oswald could move, an officer was standing before him, eyeing him coldly. "On your feet!" he barked.

Oswald stood, hands raised, and said "Well, it's all over now." Suddenly, he hit the officer in the face and drew his gun. Other officers rushed forward and grappled him to the floor. Fists flew and Oswald tasted blood in his mouth. "Don't hit me anymore!" he cried, as the officers dragged him up the aisle to the lobby. He began yelling to the patrons that he was a victim of police brutality.

"Just get him out," he heard an officer say.

"HOW COULD A MAN SHOOT THE PRESIDENT OF OUR COUNTRY?"

4

President Lyndon Johnson took the oath of office aboard Air Force One.

The air in the presidential plane felt close and hot to the new president. The air conditioning had been turned off and more and more people kept coming aboard. Johnson decided he should take the oath of office before leaving Dallas. Tradition dictated that upon the president's death, the vice president automatically became president. But Johnson wanted to make sure everything looked official in the eyes of the world, especially the Russians, America's Cold War enemy. He felt strongly that people needed to see physical proof that there had been an orderly transfer of power and that the government of the United States was stable.

Johnson summoned Sarah Hughes, a Texas federal judge he had tried to help get appointed, to swear him in. Hughes, who had been at the Trade Mart waiting for the presidential appearance, was now being rushed to Love Field. So Johnson sat with his aides and friends, waiting for the judge, Jackie Kennedy, and the casket that bore her husband.

Merriman Smith

Parkland Memorial Hospital, Dallas, 2:08 p.m.

Merriman Smith felt a hand on his shoulder. It was Jiggs Fauver of the White House transportation staff. Fauver told Smith he had been chosen to be one of three reporters to go aboard Air Force One. Smith would witness Johnson's swearing in as president and then fly back to Washington with him.

Smith left the hospital with the other two reporters, Charles Roberts of *Newsweek* and Sid Davis of Westinghouse Broadcasting, just in time to see Kilduff drive off in the press car. They spied a police officer in a squad car and pleaded with him to take them to Love Field. He complied and they hopped in as the car shot off into the midday traffic.

Clint Hill looked on as Kennedy's aides argued with the Dallas County medical examiner. The examiner was refusing to allow Kennedy's body to be removed from the hospital without an autopsy. This, he insisted, was required in all homicide cases. The aides insisted that, since this was the president's body, an autopsy could be performed back in Washington. The two sides seemed at a stalemate. Finally, the medical examiner gave in, but only on condition that a medical professional stay with the body until the autopsy was completed. Admiral George Burkley, Kennedy's personal physician, agreed to fill this role.

Hill and several other agents and aides lifted the big, bronze casket into the hearse waiting at the emergency room entrance. Then Hill gently suggested that Mrs. Kennedy ride with him to the airport in a car behind the hearse.

"No, Mr. Hill," she replied, "I'm riding with the president."

Hill opened the back door of the hearse and the two of them joined Admiral Burkley and the casket, sitting on their knees for the ride to Love Field.

Bob Schieffer
Fort Worth Police Station, 2:10 p.m.

Bob Schieffer, snap-brim detective's hat firmly on his head, was on assignment. He had been sent from the *Fort Worth Star-Telegram* newsroom to find out about a suspect in the Kennedy assassination who was being brought in. The man had pulled into a gas station in nearby Arlington and told the attendant he had heard on the radio that Kennedy had been shot. The attendant, who hadn't heard the news, assumed that anyone who knew this had to be the shooter. He quickly called the police, who rushed down to arrest the man.

All at once, the station door opened and several officers hustled in the accused man. Schieffer boldy stepped forward. He remembered a trick that the police had taught him that sometimes you can shock people into admitting the truth. So he confronted the suspect and asked him: "Why did you do it?"

The man looked at him, stunned. "Well, I didn't," he replied. After questioning the man, the police decided he wasn't involved, and quickly released him.

Clint Hill

Love Field, Dallas, 2:20 p.m.

The hearse pulled up to Air Force One. Hill and his fellow agents took out the casket and struggled up the steps of the portable staircase to the rear entrance. When they got to the top they found that the casket was too wide to fit through the narrow door. They broke off the handles and managed to jam it into the plane.

All appeared to be ready for the swearing in. Someone told Hill that Mrs. Kennedy wanted to see him in the family cabin.

As Hill entered, Kennedy took his hands in hers and looked deep into his eyes. "What's going to happen to you now, Mr. Hill?" she asked.

He couldn't believe it. Here was a woman who had just seen her husband assassinated and she was concerned about his welfare. "I'll be okay, Mrs. Kennedy," he managed to say, his voice filled with emotion. "I'll be okay."

Merriman Smith

Love Field, Dallas, 2:25 p.m.

Merriman Smith and his two colleagues pulled up in the police car just as the casket was being loaded into the plane. At the same time, Judge Hughes' car arrived. A short woman in her sixties wearing a brown dress with white polka dots, Hughes was ushered on board. Smith followed her. As he did so, he glanced down and suddenly realized he was missing something. "My God," he muttered. "I've lost my typewriter."

Lee Harvey Oswald

Dallas Police Headquarters, 2:30 p.m.

On his arrival, Oswald had not been cooperative with the police. Now sitting in Police Captain Will Fritz's office, he decided to be more compliant. Fritz asked him why he had left his place of employment, the depository, at midday.

"There was so much excitement," Oswald answered. "I just thought that there would be no more work."

After a few more questions, Oswald asked if he could get a lawyer.

"Not a problem," said Fritz. "You can call one on the pay phone on the fifth floor, but you'll have to pay for it yourself."

"I don't have any money," Oswald said.

"Then you can call collect," Fritz said.

While Oswald thought about this, Fritz asked if he'd be willing to take a polygraph test. Oswald refused and Fritz ended the interview.

Merriman Smith counted 27 people jammed together in the plane. He had never seen Air Force One so crowded. Malcolm Kilduff knelt on the floor next to Judge Hughes, ready to record the president's swearing in. White House photographer Cecil Stoughton stood on a sofa against the wall. Jackie Kennedy appeared white-faced but dry-eyed. She stood on one side of Johnson and Lady Bird stood on the other.

Johnson, his right hand upraised and his left planted on a Bible, repeated the words after Judge Hughes: "I do solemnly swear ..." It was over in a minute. Lyndon Johnson had become the 36th president of the United States when Kennedy died, but now he had been sworn in. Johnson looked around at the pale faces surrounding him. "Now let's get airborne," he said.

Jack Ruby

"It's something just unbelievable!" Jack Ruby said. "How could a man shoot the president of our country?"

Joy Dale, a dancer who worked at the club, shook her head. "Can you possibly think how Mrs. Kennedy feels?" Dale said.

Ruby, choking back tears, said, "He should be killed."

A short time later, Ruby returned to his office and phoned his sister Eva, who was his business partner. Ruby told her he was closing the clubs through the weekend. Then they discussed the latest news of the officer, J. D. Tippit, who had been gunned down in the street. Eva reported that they had caught his killer, a man named Oswald.

"He's a creep," Jack Ruby said. "He has no class."

Bob Schieffer found a chorus of phones ringing when he got back to the newsroom. He knew most of the calls would be from reporters calling in their stories on the assassination. But looking around, Schieffer saw there were few people on hand in the newsroom to take the calls.

Schieffer picked up one of the ringing phones.

A woman's voice asked, "Is there anyone there who can give me a ride to Dallas?"

Schieffer had expected to find one of his fellow reporters. Now he couldn't believe what he was hearing. "Lady, this is not a taxi, and besides, the president has been shot," he retorted.

"I know." said the woman. "They think my son is the one who shot him."

Schieffer realized with a shock that he might be speaking to the mother of the assassin. If it was indeed her, he knew the biggest story of the day had suddenly fallen into his lap.

He asked her where she lived and said he'd be right over to pick her up.

But how was he going to get her to Dallas? It didn't seem appropriate to pack her into his tiny two-seat Triumph. He went over to Bill Foster, who wrote about cars for the paper. Local car dealers regularly loaned Foster new vehicles to review for the paper. This week he had a Cadillac sedan. Schieffer asked Foster to drive him to get a story. "Come on," he said, "I'll explain as we go and you're gonna like it."

Merriman Smith
Aboard Air Force One, 4:00 p.m.

As the big plane soared eastward, Merriman Smith tapped away at a White House electric typewriter. Alongside him Charles Roberts was also working on a story. President Johnson kept stopping by their table to give them updates and to chat. First, it was to tell them he was going to make a statement shortly and would give them copies. Then, he mentioned that he had just called Rose Kennedy, the slain president's mother. Next, it was to inform them that he had called Nellie Connally at Parkland Memorial Hospital to find out how her husband was doing. While Smith appreciated Johnson's confidences, he wished he'd leave them alone to get on with their typing.

Bob Schieffer

On the road to Dallas, 4:15 p.m.

As he interviewed her in the backseat of the Cadillac, it quickly became apparent to Bob Schieffer that Marguerite Oswald wasn't a very nice person. *This is one of the most bizarre interviews I've ever had,* he thought.

Marguerite Oswald expressed no sympathy for either the dead president or her son. She only felt sorry for one person—herself. She told Schieffer that people would not feel sorry for her and that she would probably starve. She was convinced that her daughter-in-law, Marina, would get any money that came their way and all the public sympathy. Schieffer knew this would make a great story for his paper, but that an even greater story could be waiting in Dallas—an interview with Lee Harvey Oswald.

Lyndon Johnson
Aboard Air Force One, 4:35 p.m.

Lyndon Johnson could feel the tension building on the plane as it soared toward Andrews Air Force Base. In the back of the plane sat Kennedy's loyal aides, crushed by the day's events. In the front were Johnson's people, including Houston public relations executive Jack Valenti and Bill Moyers, former deputy director of the Peace Corps. The antagonism the two groups felt for one another was apparent, and nothing Johnson could say or do was likely to ease it. Johnson knew Kennedy's people saw him as a grubby, classless politician who was unworthy of filling Kennedy's shoes. But Johnson would do what he could to win them over. At least for right now, he needed them.

Schieffer ushered Marguerite Oswald into the station while Foster parked the car. The place was filled with reporters and policemen. Schieffer, in his detective's hat, had little trouble flagging down an officer. "I'm the one who brought Oswald's mother over from Fort Worth," he said. "Is there someplace she can stay where she won't be bothered by all these reporters?"

The cop led them to an interrogation room. Settling Oswald in the room, Schieffer went out to find his colleagues from the newspaper. He gathered up their stories and brought them back to the little room, which fortunately had a telephone. He began calling the stories in to the Fort Worth news desk. He smiled, realizing that never once had anyone at the police station asked him who he was.

Nellie Connally

It had been the longest afternoon of Nellie Connally's life. For the past several hours, she had waited tensely in a tiny room for word of her husband's condition. Now the surgery was over, and he had been taken to the recovery room. A doctor came in and said, "He's going to make it," and told her she could see him.

The sight of her husband shocked her. He wore an oxygen mask and a sling on his right arm. There was a tangle of tubes coming out of different parts of his body. She bent down and kissed him gently. "How is the president doing?" he asked her.

She avoided answering him. Later the doctors told her to keep Kennedy's death from him until he was stronger. Finally, the next morning, when he asked again, she told him: "the president is dead."

"I knew … " he replied in a soft, sad voice.

Bob Schieffer's luck just kept getting better. When Marina Oswald was brought into the station, an officer asked if they minded Marina joining him and Marguerite in the room. "Not at all," Schieffer told him. However, his attempts to interview Oswald's wife were frustrated because she appeared to only speak Russian.

Now, as darkness settled in, Marguerite asked Captain Fritz if she could see her son. He agreed and led her, Schieffer, Marina, and an FBI agent to a holding room. In a few minutes, Oswald would be brought into the room and Schieffer would have the interview of his career. Just then, the FBI agent turned to him and asked, "And who are you with?"

Schieffer's heart pounded in his chest. He tried to toss the question back at the other man. "Who are you with?" he responded.

The agent's eyes narrowed on him. "Are you a reporter?" he demanded.

The snap-brim hat wasn't working its magic anymore. With nothing to lose, Schieffer shot back, "Well, aren't you?"

Glaring at him, the FBI agent growled, "I'm going to kill you if I ever see you again."

Schieffer mumbled an apology and fled the room. He went back to the crowded corridor and blended in with the rest of the reporters. He'd nearly had a moment in the sun, but it was over now.

Marina (left) and Marguerite Oswald at the Dallas Police Headquarters

Jack Ruby

Dallas Police Headquarters,
November 23, 1963, 12:00 a.m.

Jack Ruby, wearing horn-rimmed glasses and clutching a notebook, entered the crowded basement of the police headquarters. Lee Harvey Oswald stood on a platform while a crush of reporters threw questions at him. Ruby, a regular at the station, had managed to sneak in.

When the questioning ended and Oswald was led away, Ruby rushed up to the platform to greet a surprised District Attorney Henry Wade.

"What are you doing here?" Wade asked.

Ruby brushed it off as a foolish question. They all knew and liked him, the officers and detectives. He was a fixture there—regularly coming by to hand out cards for his clubs, offering free admission and drinks for police officers, bringing bags of deli sandwiches for the late night crew. Before Ruby left, he chatted with an old friend, Detective August Michael

Eberhardt. "Mike," he said, "it is hard to realize that a complete nothing, a zero like that, could kill a man like President Kennedy."

Lyndon Johnson

The vice president's residence, Washington, D.C., 3:20 a.m. (EST)

It had been a 20-hour day for Lyndon Johnson. It was incredible to him that he had awakened that morning in Fort Worth as vice president and now was lying in his own bed in his pajamas as president. He had been talking from his bed for the past few hours to three of his aides—Bill Moyers, Jack Valenti, and Cliff Carter. He had gone over the agenda for the next day and used them as a sounding board. There was a lot to do. He would have his first meeting as president with Kennedy's cabinet members in the morning. He would then meet with Dwight Eisenhower, who had served as president for two terms before Kennedy. He finished talking and pulled up the bed covers. "Well, good night, boys," he said. "Get a lot of sleep fast. It's going to be a long day tomorrow."

After traveling from Andrews Air Force Base to Bethesda, Agent Hill and the Kennedy family now waited at the hospital. The autopsy had been going on for hours when agent Kellerman asked Hill to come to the autopsy room.

"I know this isn't going to be easy," Kellerman told him, "but we decided that since you are the closest to Mrs. Kennedy, it's important for you to see the body, in case she has any questions."

Hill took a deep breath and entered the room. A doctor lowered the sheet on the table, exposing the president's body. He pointed out each wound, where the bullets entered and exited. When it was over, Hill's partner, Agent Paul Landis, asked him what they had wanted. Hill explained about the possibility of Mrs. Kennedy asking him questions. "I am quite certain that will never happen," he said. Landis agreed.

Hill and the Kennedy family members watched solemnly as members of the military carried the casket into the East Room. They placed it on a funeral platform, called a catafalque. Hill had learned that it was almost identical to the one on which the coffin of assassinated President Abraham Lincoln had been laid 98 years earlier. An honor guard was placed around the catafalque.

Hill saw Jackie Kennedy and those closest to her go to the second-floor living quarters. Then he got into his car and drove to his apartment in nearby Arlington, Virginia. It was now 6:00 a.m. While his wife cooked him breakfast, he shaved, showered, and changed his clothes. After eating, he returned to his car and headed back to the White House for another long day.

Abraham Zapruder

Dal-Tex building, Dallas, 8:00 a.m.

Abe Zapruder wasn't pleased to see the man from *Life* magazine at his door. He had told Richard Stolley to come at nine, yet here he was, an hour early. But there was no point in sending him away. He would only come back again later. Zapruder was quickly learning that his film was something Stolley and many other representatives of newspapers and magazines wanted very much to get their hands on.

So he invited the man in and had him sit down

beside two Secret Service agents who were already seated in the small, windowless room. Everyone was waiting to see the premiere of Zapruder's grim home movie. The FBI had learned of the film, got it from Zapruder, and had taken it to a lab the night before to get it processed.

Zapruder now switched on the rickety projector and color images began flickering on the white wall. There was the limo. The first shot caught the president in the neck. Zapruder and his three guests watched, stunned, as they saw part of Kennedy's head blown away by the final bullet. As one, the men groaned, sickened by the sight.

Abe Zapruder now fully recognized the historic importance of his film. Because of it, he feared his life would never be quite the same again.

Clint Hill

The White House, Washington, D.C., 10:40 a.m. (EST)

The official mourning period had begun, and Clint Hill felt the family's grief as well as his own feelings of guilt. *If only I had been a little faster getting to the president's car, he might still be alive,* Hill thought.

At 10:00 a.m. there had been a private mass in the East Room for the Kennedy family. Now he accompanied Jackie Kennedy to the Oval Office. She wanted to create an inventory of the items that would be packed and taken away—her husband's rocking chair, family pictures, and other personal mementos. After she returned to her rooms, Hill took his own inventory of the events of the last two days. He wrote down details of every activity with Mrs. Kennedy. He would have to make an official report.

Abraham Zapruder
Dal-Tex building, Dallas, 11:36 a.m.

The previous night Abe Zapruder had had a terrible nightmare. In his dream, he was walking through Times Square in New York City when he saw a man standing in front of a movie house calling out, "Hey folks, come on in and see the president get killed!"

Zapruder didn't want to see his film exploited like that, yet he knew he had something of great value, something for which newspapers and magazines would pay a lot of money. Now here was Stolley from *Life* making him an offer for the film rights while a crowd of other reporters waited impatiently outside in the hall for their opportunity.

Stolley initially offered Zapruder $5,000 for the film. Zapruder made it clear that, although he needed money to secure the future of his family, he wasn't going to allow the film to be exploited. Stolley assured him that *Life* would not do that. As they talked, Stolley's offer kept going up, until he offered $50,000 for print rights to the footage.

"Let's do it," Zapruder said.

They agreed to finalize a contract in the coming days. Then Stolley slipped out the back door, leaving Zapruder to face the angry crowd in the hallway.

"I'M JACK RUBY, YOU ALL KNOW ME!"

5

Large crowds, including members of the press and police officers, gathered at the Dallas Police Headquarters to see Lee Harvey Oswald.

The shrill ring of the phone woke up Jack Ruby. It was 20-year-old Karen Carlin, one of the dancers at the Carousel Club. Carlin was calling Ruby for the third time to get an advance on her pay. Ruby was sympathetic. He knew she was four months pregnant and had a husband who couldn't find work. She needed the money.

He told her he would go downtown that morning and wire her $25 from the Western Union office. He hung up the phone, got dressed, and took one of his two pet dachschunds, Sheba, with him to the car. Ruby lived alone, had never married, and doted on his dogs like children. He drove off with $2,000 in cash in one pocket and his .38 caliber revolver in another.

Captain Will Fritz was worried. Threats had been made against the alleged assassin's life. He felt relieved when it was time to move Oswald from the city jail to the larger, less accessible county jail. He and Police Chief Jesse Curry planned for an armored truck to leave headquarters first as a decoy. After the decoy left, Oswald would be taken to a police car for the ride to the county jail. They hoped that reporters would take off in pursuit of the armored truck, thinking Oswald was in it.

Finally, everything was set and in place. All that was left to do was bring the accused man down in the elevator to the garage and then outside to the car. Fritz gave the order.

Jack Ruby

Outside Dallas Police Headquarters, 11:17 a.m.

Jack Ruby parked his car, left Sheba inside the vehicle, and headed for the Western Union office. He wired the money to Carlin and left. Just down the street was police headquarters and Ruby couldn't help but notice the large crowd gathering outside. He joined them and watched what was going on.

Lee Harvey Oswald

Dallas Police Headquarters, 11:19 a.m.

Oswald, wearing a black sweater, walked to the elevator, handcuffed to plain-clothes detective James Leavelle.

"Lee, if anybody shoots at you, I hope they're as good a shot as you are," Leavelle said.

"Aww, there ain't going to be anybody shooting at me," Oswald said. Then Oswald and Leavelle got into the elevator and began their descent to the garage.

Jack Ruby saw Patrolman Roy E. Vaughn guarding the ramp outside the police garage. The officer appeared to be preventing people or vehicles from entering. Ruby watched as Vaughn stepped away from his post to stop traffic so a car blocking the path of a patrol car could be moved. Ruby took advantage of the moment and slipped into the garage. He moved forward through the milling crowd of reporters gathered by the elevator door.

The elevator opened and Lee Harvey Oswald stepped out with officers on either side of him. Only a few feet separated Ruby from the president's killer. At that moment a man Ruby had met earlier, New York radio reporter Ike Pappas, elbowed his way forward and thrust a microphone in Oswald's face. "Do you have anything to say in your defense?" Pappas asked.

Before Oswald could speak, Ruby pulled out his revolver, took a step, and fired at Oswald's stomach, crying, "You killed the president, you rat!" Oswald doubled up in pain. Ruby saw Pappas sink to his knees as if he himself had been shot.

"There's a shot!" Pappas cried into his microphone. "Oswald has been shot! Oswald has been shot!"

In an instant a group of officers wrestled Ruby to the floor. "I'm Jack Ruby, you all know me!" he shouted.

Clint Hill

The White House, Washington, D.C., 12:30 p.m. (EST)

Clint Hill was with Special Agent in Charge (SAIC) Jerry Behn in the SAIC's East Wing office when he got an urgent phone call. General Godfrey McHugh, President Kennedy's Air Force aide, was on the line.

"Clint, I'm in the mansion and we have a problem," McHugh said. "You better get over here to the East

Room fast. Mrs. Kennedy wants to view the president."

Hill rushed over to find Jackie Kennedy in a black suit with a veil over her hair, standing by the East Room door with Bobby Kennedy. "Bobby and I want to see the president," she said.

Hill accompanied them inside and asked the honor guard to leave in order to give them some privacy. But Mrs. Kennedy said they didn't have to leave. "Just have them move away a little," she said.

Hill and McHugh moved down the flag that was draped over the casket and opened the box. Then Mrs. Kennedy asked Hill to get her a pair of scissors. He fetched them from the usher's office. After handing them over, Hill turned around and heard the sound of scissors snipping. He turned back. The Kennedys closed the casket and left. Hill returned the scissors. As he placed them in the drawer, he noticed, at the very tip, a strand of chestnut-colored hair. Mrs. Kennedy had gotten one last memento from her husband.

Malcolm Perry

Parkland Memorial Hospital, Dallas,
11:44 a.m.

As physician Malcolm Perry worked on Lee Harvey Oswald alongside two other doctors, he couldn't ignore the irony of the situation. Just a few days earlier he had worked with other doctors and staff in the attempt to save President Kennedy's life and now they were trying to do the same for his murderer.

Saving Oswald would be a daunting task. The bullet had damaged his liver, spleen, and aorta. He was also bleeding internally, but the staff members intended to do what they could to save him.

Clint Hill

The White House, Washington, D.C.,
1:08 p.m. (EST)

News of Oswald's shooting had spread fast, but Agent Hill tried to stay focused on the procession that would bring the fallen president to the U.S. Capitol.

He stood by as an honor guard carried the casket to a two-wheeled caisson pulled by six gray horses. He escorted Mrs. Kennedy and her two children, Caroline and John, to a limousine where they met the Johnsons. The limo followed the caisson up Pennsylvania Avenue. They passed hundreds of thousands of people lining the boulevard. The only sound Hill could hear was the clop-clop of horse hooves hitting the pavement and the steady beating of the military drums.

When they reached the Capitol, nine military bearers carried the casket up the 36 steps at the east side of the building. They placed the casket in the center of the Rotunda, and members of Congress paid their respects. Speaker of the House John McCormack, Chief Justice Earl Warren, and Senate Majority Leader Mike Mansfield delivered stirring eulogies. President Johnson placed a wreath at the foot of the casket. Mrs. Kennedy and Caroline knelt and kissed the flag covering the casket. Finally, Hill accompanied Mrs. Kennedy and the family back to the White House. Now it was the American people's turn to pay their respects to their fallen leader.

In her husband's hospital room, Nellie Connally became aware of a sudden tightening of security around them. She and John had watched the shooting of Oswald on the tiny television set installed in the room. Now Connally asked a passing Texas Ranger what had happened.

"Lee Harvey Oswald was just killed," he told her.

Connally felt neither sadness nor sympathy for Oswald. But she realized that history and the American people had been cheated by his untimely death. *He died before anyone could obtain any admission, any information, from him,* she thought.

Special agent Behn had a problem and, evidently, he hoped that Clint Hill could solve it for him. Behn had heard that Jackie Kennedy intended to walk in the funeral procession on Monday. If she did, Behn told Hill, the many visiting heads of states and government officials would feel compelled to walk too. This would create a security nightmare for the Secret Service.

"Will you please try to talk her out of it?" Behn pleaded. "You are the only one who even has a chance."

Hill said he would try and arranged to meet Mrs. Kennedy in the Treaty Room. When he asked her about her decision to walk she nodded. "I've decided not to walk all the way, only from the White House to St. Matthew's."

He gently told her that many other people might decide to walk if she did.

"Well, Mr. Hill, they can ride or do what they want to. I'm walking behind the president to St. Matthew's," she said.

"All right, Mrs. Kennedy," Hill replied. Afterward he phoned Behn to tell him the bad news.

"No chance to talk her out of it, Clint?" asked Behn.

"Believe me, Jerry," Hill replied. "Nothing is going to change her mind. She is walking."

6

"DEAR JACK"

Clint Hill

Agent Hill rode with Mrs. Kennedy and her brothers-in-law Bobby and Ted to the Capitol, where the president's casket lay in the Rotunda. The public viewing hours were supposed to have ended at 9:00 p.m. the previous day. But the turnout was so overwhelming that the viewing had been extended another 12 hours. By the time the Kennedys arrived, Hill heard that as many as 250,000 people had paid their respects. Hill stood by as the three Kennedys prayed beside the casket. Then an honor guard took the casket to the waiting caisson for the short ride back to the White House for the funeral.

Arriving at the White House, they found a crowd made up of the diplomatic corps and 200 foreign dignitaries from some 100 countries.

Mrs. Kennedy left her limousine and began to walk behind the caisson, her face covered by a black veil. The entire company of mourners followed her for the short walk to St. Matthew's.

Hill sat directly behind Mrs. Kennedy in the cathedral. Caroline and John sat on either side of her. It was a deeply moving requiem mass. Tenor Luigi Vena sang "Ave Maria," just as he had at the Kennedys' wedding a decade earlier. Boston's Cardinal Richard Cushing officiated. But what impressed Hill the most was how Mrs. Kennedy kept her composure during the service. Only when the cardinal referred to the late president as "dear Jack" did she start to tremble and cry. Hill placed a handkerchief in her hand and she kept it close for the remainder of the ceremony.

When the service ended, Mrs. Kennedy, John, and Caroline led the mourners out into the cold, gray afternoon. They watched the casket as it was brought out and laid again on the caisson. Members of the military gave salutes as the casket passed.

Hill saw Mrs. Kennedy lean down to John and whisper something in his ear. And little John, turning three on that day, saluted his father.

Looking around, Hill saw colonels, generals, and colleagues—some of the toughest men he knew—fighting to hold back tears.

Marina Oswald
Rose Hill Cemetery, Fort Worth, 2:13 p.m.

Marina Oswald felt that her husband's funeral had been turned into a circus. One hundred Fort Worth police officers had sealed off the cemetery to prevent curiosity seekers or troublemakers from interrupting the service. Marina Oswald couldn't help but think that if security for her husband had been this tight earlier, he might still be alive.

The police, however, hadn't kept out the throng of reporters and photographers who stood about, staring and taking pictures of her, Marguerite, her two children, and Lee's older brother, Robert—the only people here who she actually knew. She watched, dry-eyed, as several reporters, recruited to be pallbearers, carried the simple pine coffin to the graveside. Then the head of the Fort Worth Council of Churches—another volunteer, since the designated minister never arrived—delivered a brief, simple sermon. When he finished, Oswald went up to the open coffin and took off her wedding ring. She tried to slip it on Lee's finger, but it wouldn't fit. So she gently placed it in the coffin and turned away. Secret Service agents escorted her to a waiting car.

Clint Hill

Arlington National Cemetery, Virginia, 2:50 p.m.

Soon after he arrived with the other mourners at the Kennedy gravesite, Agent Hill looked up and saw about 50 Air Force and Navy planes flying overhead. Then another plane's sound was heard. The sound seemed familiar to Hill, the high-pitched whine of a perfectly tuned set of jet engines. It was Air Force One flying by low. Hill watched as the pilot dipped the plane's wings in salute.

After the brief ceremony, Mrs. Kennedy was handed a lighted torch and touched it to a gas-fueled device, the Eternal Flame. She had asked for one just like the flame that burned at the Tomb of the Unknown Soldier in Paris, France. As the flame shot up, she passed the torch to Bobby Kennedy and then to his brother, Ted.

A bugler played Taps, the traditional ending to a military funeral. He flubbed one note, probably due to nervousness on this great occasion. Hill felt sorry for the bugler. *He will never forget it, and the world has it recorded for posterity,* he thought.

Lyndon Johnson
Washington, D.C., 5:20 p.m. (EST)

President Johnson's right hand was beginning to feel numb. He had been shaking the hands of foreign dignitaries for 20 minutes in a reception line following the funeral. As Secretary of State Dean Rusk introduced each new person to the president, an assistant secretary whispered information on that person into Johnson's ear.

The hand shaking was nearly at an end as the guests moved into the John Quincy Adams Room for a buffet dinner. Johnson massaged his right hand and prepared himself for 16 brief, personal encounters with select leaders of state in the Thomas Jefferson Room. Then he would leave the reception and head back to the White House to meet with 35 state governors in the Executive Office Building. That would be followed by a budget meeting at 8:45 p.m. The new president knew he was hitting the ground running, but he would have it no other way.

Clint Hill

The White House, Washington, D.C., November 26, 1963, 12:00 a.m. (EST)

An exhausted Clint Hill was sitting in the Map Room, about to call it a day, when the phone rang. It was Jackie Kennedy. "Mr. Hill, Bobby and I want to go to Arlington now. We want to see the flame."

Hill said he would get the car. As they crossed the Memorial Bridge, they could see the bright flame flickering through the darkness. When they reached the cemetery, Mrs. Kennedy got out, carrying a small bouquet of flowers. She placed it on the grave and knelt in silent prayer with her brother-in-law. Then they all got into the car and rode back through the chilly night to the White House.

An eternal flame was placed at President Kennedy's gravesite at Jackie Kennedy's request.

EPILOGUE

The assassination of President Kennedy remains one of the darkest events in American history. It brought an end to a presidency that had captured the nation's imagination and the adoration of many. The event was widely seen as the end of an age of innocence and idealism in American life.

In addition, Kennedy's assassination helped make television the media giant and news source it remains to this day. Before November 22, 1963, most Americans got their news from newspapers and radio rather than television. In the days after the assassination, television's power grew. Suspending all regular programming through the president's funeral, the three television networks became the gathering place for a nation of mourners. Televisions in about 93 percent of American homes were tuned to the funeral. Millions also watched, stunned, as Lee Harvey Oswald was shot live on television by Jack Ruby.

Lee Harvey Oswald was determined to have been the sole assassin of Kennedy by the 1964

Warren Commission. The commission was established by President Johnson to investigate the assassination. However, conspiracy theories that say Oswald did not act alone, or was set up for the murder, persist to this day.

Marina Oswald married Dallas carpenter Kenneth Porter in 1965 and had a son with him. She continues to live in Rockwall, Texas, with her husband today.

Marguerite Oswald died in 1981, not having spoken to her former daughter-in-law for years.

Bob Schieffer was hired by CBS News in 1969. He enjoyed a long career, serving the television network as its chief Washington correspondent, anchor of the Saturday edition of the evening news, and the moderator of its Sunday news program *Face the Nation* from 1991 until his retirement in 2015.

President Lyndon Johnson was re-elected for a full term by a landslide in 1964. Johnson was able to push through much of the legislation that Kennedy had proposed, including the Civil Rights Act of 1964. He also became embroiled in the Vietnam War. The war became so unpopular with the American public that Johnson declined to run for a second full term in March 1968. Lyndon Johnson died of a heart attack on January 22, 1973.

Abraham Zapruder donated $25,000 of the money he earned from the rights to his film to the widow of J. D. Tippit, the police officer who was killed by Lee Harvey Oswald. Zapruder died of stomach cancer in 1970 in Dallas. In 1975 Time, Inc., publisher of *Life*, sold back the rights to his film to his family for $1. Three years later, the Zapruder family allowed the film to be stored at the National Archives and Records Administration, where it remains today.

Nellie Connally remained First Lady of Texas until 1969, when her husband left the governorship. He was later secretary of the Treasury in the administration of President Richard Nixon. John Connally died in 1993. Nellie Connally wrote a memoir about the Kennedy assassination, *From Love Field*, which was published in 2003. She died three years later.

Clint Hill continued as Secret Service agent to Jackie Kennedy until after the 1964 presidential election. Then he was assigned to protect President Johnson and, later, President Richard Nixon's vice president, Spiro Agnew. Hill retired from the Secret Service in 1975. He has written two memoirs, *Mrs. Kennedy and Me* (2012) and *Five Days in November* (2013). Today he resides near San Francisco, one of the few key participants of that tragic day still living.

Merriman Smith won a Pulitzer Prize in Journalism in 1964 for his coverage of the Kennedy assassination. He was awarded the Presidential Medal of Freedom by President Johnson in 1967. Smith, despondent over the death of his son in the Vietnam War, shot himself in 1970. He is buried in Arlington National Cemetery alongside his son.

Jack Ruby was found guilty of the murder of Lee Harvey Oswald on March 14, 1964, and was sentenced to death. In October 1966, the Texas Court of Criminal Appeals reversed the conviction due to judicial errors and ordered a new trial for Ruby. Before the trial could start, however, Ruby died of cancer at Parkland Memorial Hospital in Dallas.

TIMELINE

8:50 A.M.: President John F. Kennedy addresses 5,000 union members in a parking lot in Fort Worth, Texas.

11:25 A.M.: Air Force One takes off from Carlswell Air Force Base for the short flight to Love Field in Dallas.

11:55 A.M.: The presidential motorcade leaves Love Field and heads for downtown Dallas.

12:30 P.M.: Lee Harvey Oswald shoots President Kennedy and Texas governor John Connally from the Texas School Book Depository.

12:38 P.M.: The presidential limo arrives at Parkland Memorial Hospital and both Kennedy and Connally are rushed into the emergency room.

1:00 P.M.: President Kennedy is pronounced dead, although the official announcement is not made to the press for another half hour.

1:15 P.M.: On the street, Oswald is confronted by Officer J. D. Tippit and fatally shoots him.

1:26 P.M.: President Lyndon Johnson leaves Parkland Memorial Hospital for Air Force One.

1:33 P.M.: Malcolm Kilduff announces that the president is dead.

1:50 P.M.: Oswald is apprehended in a local movie house by police.

2:38 P.M.: Johnson is sworn in as president aboard Air Force One by Judge Sarah Hughes and the plane quickly takes off.

4:00 P.M.: Reporter Bob Schieffer picks up Marguerite Oswald and interviews her on the drive to Dallas to see her son.

6:05 P.M. (EST): Air Force One lands at Andrews Air Force Base, where Robert Kennedy is the first person to come aboard.

6:14 P.M. (EST): Johnson delivers his first statement as president at the base.

8:00 P.M. (EST): Doctors at Bethesda Naval Hospital begin an autopsy on Kennedy.

November 23, 1963

12:00 A.M.: Dallas police conduct a chaotic press conference with Oswald and reporters in police headquarters. Jack Ruby is present.

4:24 A.M. (EST): Kennedy's body arrives at the White House after the autopsy and is placed in the East Room of the mansion.

8 A.M.: Zapruder shows his film of the assassination for the first time in his office to two Secret Service agents and Richard Stolley of *Life* magazine.

10:45 A.M. (EST): Mrs. Kennedy, following a mass in the East Room, begins to go through her husband's things in the Oval Office.

2 P.M. (EST): Mrs. Kennedy and Bobby Kennedy choose a gravesite for the president at Arlington National Cemetery.

November 24, 1963

11:21 A.M.: Jack Ruby shoots Oswald as he is being moved from the city to the county jail.

11:44 A.M.: Oswald arrives at Parkland Memorial Hospital, the same hospital where Kennedy died two days earlier.

1:07 P.M.: Oswald is pronounced dead.

9:00 P.M. (EST): The president's casket is put on display in the Capitol Rotunda and the public is allowed in to pay its respects.

November 25, 1963

9 A.M. (EST): The president's casket is moved out of the Rotunda and back on the caisson to return to the White House.

11:35 A.M. (EST): Mrs. Kennedy leads the procession on foot from the White House to St. Matthew's Cathedral.

2:13 P.M.: Lee Harvey Oswald's funeral service begins at Rose Hill Cemetery in Fort Worth.

2:40 P.M. (EST): Mourners arrive at Arlington for the president's burial. Mrs. Kennedy lights the Eternal Flame.

5:00 P.M. (EST): President Johnson presides over a reception for foreign dignitaries at the State Department.

GLOSSARY

autopsy (AW-top-see)—an examination performed on a dead body to find the cause of death

caisson (KAY-son)—a two-wheeled wagon used for carrying heavy ammunition

catafalque (CAT-uh-fahlk)—a round structure on which a dead person's body lies in state

defect (di-FEKT)—desert a country for another

entourage (ahn-too-RAHZH)—people who travel with a high-ranking person

eulogy (YOO-luh-jee)—a speech to honor a dead person

gurney (GUR-nee)—a wheeled table or stretcher for carrying patients or bodies in a hospital

rotunda (roh-TUN-duh)—a large, circular room with a dome above; when capitalized, it refers specifically to the Rotunda in the Capitol building in Washington, D.C.

CRITICAL THINKING USING THE COMMON CORE

1. Many people have speculated about what would have happened if President Kennedy had not been killed on November 22, 1963. Would he have been re-elected? What might he have achieved in a second term? Would American history in the 1960s and beyond have been different? Explain. (Integration of Knowledge and Ideas)

2. Looking back, we can't help but wonder if the assassination could have been prevented if events had taken a different turn. What events and incidents contributed to this tragedy? What role did the Secret Service, President Kennedy himself, and other individuals play in the way things turned out? (Craft and Structure)

3. Although the Warren Commission and other investigations into the assassination make a powerful case for Oswald being the sole assassin of the president, conspiracy theories of all kinds continue to abound more than 50 years after the event. Why do you think this is? Why do so many people find it difficult to accept that Oswald killed Kennedy and that he did it alone? (Integration of Knowledge and Ideas)

INTERNET SITES

FactHound offers a safe, fun way to find Internet sites related to this book. All of the sites on FactHound have been researched by our staff.

Here's all you do:
Visit *www.facthound.com*
Type in this code: 9781491484517

FactHound will fetch the best sites for you!

FURTHER READING

Burgan, Michael. *John F. Kennedy*. Chicago: Heinemann Library, 2013.

Collins, Terry. *The Assassination of John F. Kennedy, November 22, 1963*. Chicago: Heinemann Library, 2014.

Nardo, Don. *Assassination and Its Aftermath: How a Photograph Reassured a Shocked Nation*. North Mankato, Minnesota: Compass Point Books, 2014.

Norwich, Grace. *I Am John F. Kennedy*. New York: Scholastic Inc., 2013.

Senker, Cath. *Kennedy and the Cuban Missile Crisis*. Chicago: Heinemann Library, 2014.

Swanson, James. L. *"The President Has Been Shot!": The Assassination of John F. Kennedy*. New York: Scholastic Press, 2013.

SELECTED BIBLIOGRAPHY

Belli, Melvin M. *Dallas Justice: The Real Story of Jack Ruby and His Trial.* New York: McKay, 1964.

Bishop, Jim. *The Day Kennedy Was Shot.* New York: Funk & Wagnalls, 1968.

Caro, Robert A. *The Passage of Power.* New York: Vintage Books, A division of Random House, Inc., 2013.

Connally, Nellie, and Mickey Herskowitz. *From Love Field: Our Final Hours with President John F. Kennedy.* New York: Rugged Land, 2003.

Hill, Clint, with Lisa McCubbin. *Mrs. Kennedy and Me.* New York: Gallery Books, 2012.

Manchester, William. *The Death of a President, November 20– November 25, 1963.* New York: Harper & Row, 1967.

Schieffer, Bob. *This Just In: What I Couldn't Tell You on TV.* New York: G. P. Putnam's Son, 2003.

Trost, Cathy, and Susan Bennett. *President Kennedy Has Been Shot.* Naperville, IL: Sourcebooks Mediafusion, 2003.

INDEX

ABOUT THE AUTHOR

Steven Otfinoski has written more than 170 books for young readers. His previous book in the Tangled History series is *Day of Infamy*. Among his many other books for Capstone is the You Choose book *The Sinking of the Lusitania*. Three of his nonfiction books have been named Books for the Teen Age by the New York Public Library. He lives in Connecticut with his family.